Mi Mysteries 3

20 more Tricky Tales to Untangle

By Rick Walton

Illustrated by Lauren Scheuer

★ American Girl®

Published by American Girl Publishing, Inc.

Copyright © 2007 by American Girl, LLC

Questions or comments? Call 1-800-845-0005, visit our Web site at **americangirl.com**, or write to Customer Service, American Girl, 8400 Fair way Place, Middleton, WI 53562-0497.

Printed in China

07 08 09 10 11 12 LEO 10 9 8 7 6 5 4 3 2

All American Girl marks are trademarks of American Girl, LLC.

Editorial Development: Trula Magruder
Art Direction & Design: Chris Lorette David
Production: Mindy Rappe, Lisa Bunescu, Jeannette Bailey, Judith Lary
Illustrations: Lauren Scheuer

Dear Reader,

Just when you think Marie and her pals can't possibly crack another case, they're back on the job! This time, Marie and Noelle need cash—lots of it—to fly to Hawaii. Unfortunately, they'll face 20 mysteries before the year's up. Will they make it to Hawaii? Will new suspects force them to postpone their plans? Will a real crime be more than the duo can handle?

Follow Marie and her pals and see if you can be the first to figure out whodunit! Once you think you've found a solution, open the "case closed" folder in back.

Happy sleuthing!

Your friends at American Girl

MARIE

Contents

NOELLE

Sage

Rose

FAith

HOpE

BRooKe

HAiLeY

The Sisterhood and the Traveling Aunt

Marie's aunt offers a trip of a lifetime.
Will bad news end someone's dream?

"We're going to Hawaii! We're going to Hawaii!" Marie told her best friend, Noelle.

"Cool!" Noelle said.

Noelle tossed her work gloves in with the dirty clothes. She had just planted a bed of dahlias under her dad's window. Noelle and her mom had planned this surprise so that her father's favorite flowers would bloom for his birthday in September.

"What a lucky family! I wish I could go," said Noelle.

"No," Marie said. "The 'we' is you and me! *We* are going to Hawaii. My aunt Kristine visited us this weekend. She's traveled to Bali and Tahiti and recently she flew to—"

"Marie!" Noelle shouted.

"Well, my aunt plans to take us with her to Hawaii!"

Noelle stared in shock at Marie for a second and then screamed, "No way!"

"But there's a catch," Marie said.

"I knew it was too good to be true," Noelle said.

"Oh, this is still good," added Marie. "Aunt Kristine believes that kids should learn responsibility. So she insists we earn half the cost of our expenses. She'll pay the rest."

"How much will we need to earn?" Noelle asked.

Marie told her.

Noelle whistled. "That's a lot of money. Do you think we can do it?"

"I think so," said Marie. "I've already brainstormed ideas with my parents. They know people who will hire us for small jobs."

Suddenly, Noelle jumped into the air, waving her arms. "We're going to Hawaii! We're going to Hawaii!"

"So that's where we're moving?" asked Noelle's brother, Nicholas, as he sauntered into the room. "I thought we were moving to New England. But I like Hawaii, too. I'll become a famous surfer."

Noelle stared at Nicholas. "What do you mean, 'So that's where we're moving'?"

"Didn't Mom and Dad tell you?" Nicholas asked. "We're moving as soon as school's out for the summer. I heard them talking about it."

"We can't be moving!" Noelle said.

"We can't, but we are," said Nicholas. He plopped onto the sofa and reached for the remote.

"Dad must've heard from that company he mentioned a while back," Noelle said. "Well, I'm not moving. I'll stay with Marie—unless Marie wants to come live with us in New England or wherever we're going. That would be good, too. In fact, I'll talk to Mom and Dad right now. Where are they?"

"Shopping," Nicholas said. "I only heard about all this myself just before they left. They didn't know I was listening. I think it's a surprise."

"Some surprise," said Noelle.

"What exactly did they say?" Marie questioned.

"Let's see." Nicholas thought for a minute. "Mom said we'd love New England, but she worried that the house would be too small. And then Dad said he had a lot to do before we left, like placing the mail on hold at the post office and telling all the neighbors that we'll be leaving soon. And they both said a lot of other things, but I can't remember them."

"You did just fine," Marie said. "Except for the part where you thought your family was moving. Noelle, you'll still be my best friend, you'll still live next door, and we're still traveling to Hawaii together!"

The Sisterhood and the Traveling Aunt

How did Marie know that Noelle wasn't moving?
For a move in the right direction, turn to page 81.

Light Housekeeping

A dragon banister and a creaking door—have Marie and Noelle's moneymaking plans gone too far?

After Aunt Kristine left, it didn't take the girls long to find work. Noelle's mom knew the caretaker of a large historic home that opened for tours only during the summer months.

The caretaker, Mrs. Peterson, had hired Marie and Noelle to help clean the mansion before the tours began. The instant the friends stepped into the foyer of the elegant home, they realized what a big job cleaning it would be.

"Welcome, girls!" hailed Mrs. Peterson as she tap-tap-tapped across the glossy floor. "While I'm checking for cleaning materials, I've asked Gwen to show you around. She's training to be a tour guide and would like the practice."

"Hi! I'm Gwen," the older teen said. She stepped forward and changed to her tour-guide voice: "Let's start in the Great Hall, shall we?"

Gwen opened a door and flipped a switch. Electric lightbulbs on the chandelier lit up a thousand teardrop-shaped crystals, filling the room with light. Large chairs, sofas, ornamental tables, and statues furnished every corner.

"The owners held town meetings, dances, and banquets in this room. People loved the parties here."

"I'd have a party every night," Noelle said to Marie as she ran her hand along an enormous fireplace mantel. She held up her fingers. "Not much dust. This should be easy."

"If we were just cleaning *this* room," said Marie. "But this place will take forever."

Gwen led the girls through the house, pointing out interesting details. "Artisans hand-carved this banister. Notice the glass eyes of the dragons. Aren't they beautiful?"

"Beautiful and creepy," Marie whispered to Noelle.

"And here we have the dining room. The family shipped the table from Italy and the grandfather clock from France."

Gwen flipped a switch next to a cabinet, and suddenly green-and-white china sparkled on the shelves. "Even the kids knew to be careful with these treasures."

"I hope we don't break anything, either. That would cut into our savings for Hawaii," Noelle said.

"Good point," Marie replied. "Maybe we should just clean things that can't be knocked over or moved."

"That leaves the floor," joked Noelle.

"Imagine yourself gliding into this room for your first party," said Gwen, recalling a line in a script she had obviously worked hard to memorize. "You see this house—this room—*exactly* as it was two hundred years ago."

While the three girls imagined themselves in the past, the only sound they could hear was a ticking clock.

"We need to go," said Gwen quickly.

"Why?" asked Marie.

"I need to show you something I've never shown to anyone before today."

"Where's Mrs. Peterson?" asked Noelle. "Shouldn't we get to work?"

"This is more important." Gwen led the girls from room to room until they arrived at a door. "You won't believe this!"

Slowly Gwen opened the door. She cracked open the door, slid her hand inside, flipped a switch, and screamed.

"Ah!" yelled Noelle and Marie as bright light poured over shelves stocked with cleaning supplies. All three laughed.

"Did you enjoy the tour?" Mrs. Peterson asked. She stepped from a small office into the room with the girls.

"Loved it!" Noelle exclaimed.

"And Gwen's a great tour guide," said Marie. "She excites you about the house. But she did have one small error in her tour script." Marie smiled at the teen.

"She did?" asked Mrs. Peterson.

"I did?" Gwen looked confused. And then she smiled. "Oh, yeah! Good catch. I noticed that on my first day and forgot to change it."

Light
Housekeeping

Exactly what did Marie catch?
To cast a little light on the subject, turn to page 81.

Stocks in a Box

A diary leads the girls to real buried treasure.
But can they solve a mystery this old?

"Have you ever read what your mom wrote in her diary when she was a kid?" Noelle asked Marie over the phone on the last Saturday in May.

"My mom didn't keep a diary," Marie said.

"You can learn a lot of interesting things. Come over and I'll show you something I read in Mom's."

Marie picked up two apples from the fruit bowl, walked over to Noelle's house, and knocked on her door.

"I'm in the den!" shouted Noelle. "Come in."

Marie walked into the den to see Noelle standing next to a bookshelf, holding up an old diary. "My mom's."

"She lets you read it?" Marie asked. She placed the apples on a shelf and leaned over Noelle's shoulder.

"She thinks it brings us closer together," said Noelle. "And you know? It does. But this is the part I wanted you to see." She held out the diary. Marie read aloud from it.

July 24

Today's my 9th birthday. Mom and Dad took me to Lulu's for lunch. Grandpa gave me 10 shares of Honeysuckle stock (whatever that means). He said to put it someplace safe, so I put it in a tin and buried it where the church steeple pointed at two o'clock. Someday, when I'm older, I'll dig it up.

"Wow!" Marie said. "Honeysuckle is a big company. Could the stock be worth a lot of money?"

"Let's go ask my mom if she ever dug it up," Noelle said. The girls skipped to Mrs. Dee's home office and tapped on her door.

"Come in, girls!" Mrs. Dee said, laughing. "I could hear you coming a mile away."

After the girls showed Mrs. Dee the diary passage, she didn't say a word for a moment. "I don't even remember this," she said, nearly whispering. "Stocks didn't mean anything to me, so I blocked them out of my mind."

"You don't remember digging up the tin? It might still be there?" Noelle asked.

"Could be." Mrs. Dee grinned. "Imagine that!"

"In that case, what kind of reward would you give two girls if they found it for you?" Noelle said.

"What reward would you suggest?" Mrs. Dee asked.

"Donating it to the 'Send Noelle and Marie to Hawaii Fund'?" Noelle suggested.

"I'll tell you what," said Mrs. Dee. "If you find the stocks, you can have half of the value. With the rest, I'll buy some earplugs." She laughed and rubbed Noelle's head.

"It's a deal!" Noelle said. "Marie, we have a box of stocks to find."

Mrs. Dee agreed to drive the girls to the house where she grew up. Her parents, Noelle's Grandma and Grandpa Ivy, still lived there. The couple walked out to the driveway ready to dole out hugs as soon as they saw their daughter drive up.

"To what do we owe this surprise?" asked Grandpa Ivy.

Noelle told him the story of the stocks.

"That was my dad . . . and my daughter," said Grandpa Ivy. He laughed. "Why are we waiting? Let's go dig up the box!"

"Mom, show us where you buried your treasure."

Mrs. Dee glanced around the yard. "I have no idea," she said. "I'm sorry."

"Just dig up the whole yard," said Grandma Ivy. "I've begged your grandpa to redo the landscaping. This will make him do it."

"Wait," said Noelle. "Mom, your diary gave us a clue where to look." She pointed to the church next door. "We just need to wait until two o'clock."

"I'll fix us some lunch while we wait," said Grandma Ivy.

At 1:45 P.M. everyone stepped outside for the magic hour. Noelle and Marie, holding their shovels, watched as the steeple shadow moved slowly across the yard. Grandpa Ivy kept track of the time. At exactly 2:00 P.M., he shouted, "Now!"

At that exact moment, Noelle stuck her shovel into the ground right where the point of the steeple shadow hit the yard—between Grandma's garden gnome and a giant oak tree.

The girls and Grandpa Ivy dug, and they dug, and they dug deeper, and they dug wider.

And nothing.

They found no box.

They found no stocks.

"I'm sorry," said Mrs. Dee. "I probably dug them up and forgot about it. Or I never buried them. They're not here."

"But we do have the makings of a mighty fine swimming pool," said Grandma Ivy.

Just then Marie shouted, "Of course they're not here. If I had paid attention, we could've saved ourselves tons of work."

"What do you mean?" Noelle asked. "Where are they?"

"We forgot a very important detail," Marie said.

Stocks in a Box

What was the detail the crew forgot?
Turn to page 81 to dig into the answer.

Time to Shape Up

Hope claims to be jealous of Marie and Noelle's trip. Will her feelings interfere with their plans?

"I just thought of something, Marie," Noelle said on the Friday morning after school was out for the summer.

The girls arrived at Marie's house ready to make summer plans that didn't involve too much thinking.

"You thought what?" asked Marie.

"It's just that I realized we'll be in Hawaii before long."

"That again?" said Faith. "What about today?"

"As I was saying," said Noelle to Marie. "Surfing? Swimming? Hiking?"

"Isn't it great?" smiled Marie.

"It will be," said Hope, "but you two are so out of shape, you'll kill yourselves!" Ever since Hope had heard about the trip, she had known how much fun Marie and Noelle would have. She had traveled to Hawaii with her parents two years ago and could still remember every detail.

"Exactly what I'm trying to say," added Noelle.

"What do you mean, 'out of shape'?" Marie asked. She flexed her biceps.

"You're in walk-around-the-mall shape," said Hope. "Not in climb-to-the-top-of-a-tropical-mountain shape. Trust me! I ached after my first day there."

"We're not ready," said Noelle.

"You may be right," Marie said. "So what should we do?"

"You walk," said Noelle. "We walk." Noelle waved her hands in a circle to include everyone in the group.

"Walk!" the girls all shouted.

"What if we walk to get ice cream at Moo's?" asked Rose.

"Or walk to the pool. I've bought the cutest swimsuit!" added Brooke. "It's red, white, and blue."

"Let's start tomorrow," said Noelle. "Everyone come to my house for a sleepover, and we'll get up early and hike."

"We're not going to Hawaii," the other girls moaned.

"But we are supporting our friends," said Hope.

At 9:00 P.M. after sandwiches and sodas, Noelle announced, "O.K. It's time for bed so that we can wake up early."

"I'm not tired," Brooke said.

"Me neither," added Faith.

"Scrabble?" Marie asked. She pulled out two game boards. "That will tire our brains and make us sleepy."

After four Scrabble games, Marie said, "I'm tired *now.*"

"Me too," Noelle said. "I could sleep through a tornado."

"Could be a problem," said Sage. "How do we wake up?"

"Do you have an alarm clock, Noelle?" asked Hope.

"On the dresser," she muttered.

Hope walked over to the dresser and Marie followed. They stared at the digital clock. "It's 1:36 A.M.!" Marie shouted.

Hope pushed the Alarm Set button. The clock blinked: 12:00 . . . 12:00 . . . 12:00 . . . 12:00 . . .

"Six A.M.?" Hope asked.

"I'm tired thinking about it," said Rose, "but if we must."

Marie watched Hope set the alarm. The lights flashed 1:00 . . . 2:00 . . . 3:00 . . . 4:00 . . . 5:00 . . . 6:00 . . . 7:00 . . . "Whoops, missed it," Hope said to herself. She continued to press the button and the numbers flickered from 8 past 12 and back to 6. "There!"

"Be sure you switch on the alarm," Noelle said.

Hope switched on the alarm.

"Electrical cord plugged in?" Noelle asked.

"Of course," Hope said. "You really *are* tired."

And within a few minutes, all the girls were asleep.

When Marie woke up, she felt great. The sun was shining and she had woken up naturally.

Naturally? No alarm? She looked at the clock: 10:14.

"Uh, Noelle, Hope . . ." Marie said.

"What?" Noelle asked, covering her head with a pillow.

"It's after six!"

Noelle jumped up. "How much after?"

"It's almost time for lunch."

"Did we sleep through the alarm?" asked Faith.

"Alarms wake me up," Brooke said. "Is your clock broken?"

"I don't think so," Noelle said. She got up to check. "Looks O.K. to me."

Brooke teased, "Has someone's jealousy gone too far?"

"You're right," added Rose. "Hope, how could you?"

"Did the power go off in the night?" asked Hope.

Noelle looked at her watch. "No, my watch has the same time as the clock."

"I swear I didn't do this on purpose," said Hope.

Marie looked more closely at the clock. "It was you, Hope," said Marie. "But I doubt it happened because of jealousy."

Time to Shape Up

What did Marie know?
Time to find out. Turn to page 81.

What a Character!

A great job awaits the girls—if they can find the right location. Will they make it on time?

"You two owe me big-time!" Brooke told Marie and Noelle as they gathered up tools. Brooke's grandmother had a friend, Mrs. Allen, who needed yard work done. She had a big yard and promised to pay the girls well if they did a good job.

"Sure," Noelle said. "Next time Dad asks me to mow our lawn, you'll be the first one I call." She smiled and then said, "But really, thanks for asking us to help."

"Especially if we do a good job," Brooke said. "Grandma says Mrs. Allen might ask us back every week."

"Ready?" Mrs. Cantu asked from behind the wheel of the van. She had volunteered to drive the girls.

"Almost, Mom," Marie said. The girls put the last of the tools in the back and piled into the van.

"Buckle up!" Mrs. Cantu shouted, as she always did just before her van set off. "Now, give me the address."

"It's . . . oh . . . 333 something," Brooke said.

"Well, that narrows it down for us," Mrs. Cantu said under her breath.

"Mrs. Allen said to head down Ninth Avenue," added Brooke. "Maybe I'll know the street when I see it."

"Don't you remember anything about the name?" Mrs. Cantu asked. "What letter does it start with?"

"The name reminded me of a children's book character," Brooke said. "But I can't remember which one."

"I don't know any streets around here named after book characters," said Mrs. Cantu, sounding a bit more stressed.

"It wasn't a character. It was *almost* a character."

"Wonderful," said Mrs. Cantu sarcastically. The way she said "wonderful" made the girls burst out laughing.

"It's not smart to show up late on your first day," said Noelle. She was stressed, too. With only a short time left before summer ended, Noelle worried whether she and Marie could earn enough to afford Hawaii.

"Madeleine Street?" asked Marie. "Lois Lane?"

This put everyone in the right mood. The girls threw out names of other famous book characters.

"No," Brooke said, feeling frustrated.

"Well, here's Ninth," said Mrs. Cantu. "Start looking."

The girls shouted out the street names as they passed each sign.

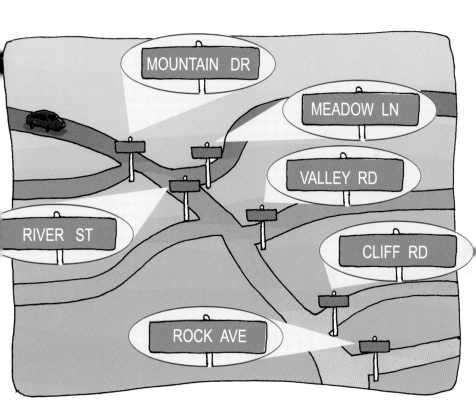

Suddenly Marie shouted, "Stop!"

Mrs. Cantu slammed on the brakes. "What's wrong?"

"Turn around!" Marie exclaimed. "I know where it is!"

What a Character!

Where is it?
To head in the right direction, turn to page 81.

Incredible Ice Cream

A hot day zaps the girls' motivation to work—until
Mrs. Ferris finds a frosty solution.

"Is it just me, or does it feel like we're on fire?" Noelle
asked from behind a pile of sweet corn at the Farmers' Market.

Hailey's mom had hired the girls to sell vegetables from
the Ferrises' garden and gifts from the family's import business.

"Next time I'll bring a canopy," said Mrs. Ferris. "I didn't
expect it to be so hot today."

Noelle took a long swallow from her water bottle, finishing it off. "I'm going to fill up my bottle again. Anyone?"

"Everyone should refill," said Mrs. Ferris. "We don't want anyone to overheat."

Noelle collected all the bottles and headed to find a faucet.

On her return, the girls watched Noelle wind her way around people and stalls, twisting and turning like a snake to prevent a single bottle from dropping to the pavement.

"Thanks for the help, guys," a dripping-wet Noelle said.

Mrs. Ferris snapped Noelle's picture, and then the girls laughed as each one grabbed her bottle.

"It looks as if yours is on your head," Marie said.

"I stuck my head under a faucet," Noelle said. "The only thing I need now is ice cream from the snack bar."

"How much?" Marie asked, reaching into her pocket.

"Three dollars for an ice cream sandwich."

"Three dollars!" Marie, Hailey, and Hope said in unison.

"They have a captive audience today," grumbled Noelle.

"I'm tempted," Marie said. "But it would take a huge chunk out of what we're earning today."

"Tough decision," said Noelle. "Buy overpriced ice cream here, or wait and buy overpriced ice cream in Hawaii."

All the ice cream talk made the girls hungry. They lifted the cooler onto the table and dug through it for their lunches.

After eating, all the girls moved like overfed snakes. They slowly picked up their garbage and dragged to their workstations.

"You girls need more water," said Mrs. Ferris. "I'll make the water run this time."

The girls handed her their bottles, and she headed off.

Several minutes later Mrs. Ferris returned. She passed out the water, and then laid a plastic bag on the table.

"Ice cream sandwiches!" the girls shouted.

"You needn't do this," said Hope. "It'll eat up the profits."

"Don't worry," Mrs. Ferris said. "I picked them up at the store this morning and kept them in the back of our air-conditioned van. I just remembered when I went for water."

"This tastes good!" said Noelle. "And soooo cold! I really needed it."

After the girls ate their ice cream, they felt energized. They helped customers and rearranged vegetables.

"Thanks for the treat," Marie whispered to Mrs. Ferris. "I know you bought the ice cream here at the market."

"You're good workers and deserve it," Mrs. Ferris said. "Nothing slips by you, does it?"

Incredible
Ice Cream

Did it slip by you?
For the cold, hard truth, turn to page 81.

What's for Dinner?

Four meals mean trouble for two babysitters. Will the sitters make the correct dinner decision?

"Ethan and Ellen shouldn't be any trouble," said Mrs. Lloyd on the phone to Marie. "Excuse me a second—"

"—Brent," Mrs. Lloyd said, muffling the phone with her hand, "please take out the kitchen garbage. It's overflowing. Thank you! Thank you! Thank you!—Now, where was I?" Mrs. Lloyd asked, returning to Marie.

"You said the twins won't be any trouble," Marie said.

"Oh, yeah. Put them to bed at eight, read a couple of stories, and they'll go right to sleep. We'll leave out their favorite toys and DVDs. I can't believe I'm going to see a movie with company coming tomorrow for lunch. At least I've prepared all the food already."

"Everything will be fine, Mrs. Lloyd."

"I'll cook something for you, too. I'll leave it in the fridge. Just heat it in the microwave. Noelle's coming, right?"

"I haven't asked. I believe she's free, if you don't mind."

"No problem. When caring for twins, four hands are better than two. I'll stick our cell-phone number on the fridge in case of emergency," Mrs. Lloyd said. "See you at five!"

At a quarter to five, Marie and Noelle arrived at the Lloyd house. The girls waited while Mrs. Lloyd rushed around attending to last-minute details.

"I'll keep my cell phone on vibrate," she said.

The Lloyds kissed their five-year-olds good-bye and left.

The girls adored the twins. Ellen told silly jokes. Ethan made funny noises. And both of them laughed a lot.

Noelle taught the kids to do somersaults, and Ellen taught Marie and Noelle how to count to one hundred.

At six o'clock Noelle said, "Is it time for dinner?"

"My stomach says 'yes,'" said Marie. "What do you think, kids?"

"My stomach says 'yes, yes, yes!'" said Ethan, and he ran to the kitchen and threw open the refrigerator door.

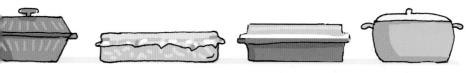

Four serving dishes sat on the top shelf. Marie looked into each dish. Roast beef filled one, roast chicken another, spaghetti and meatballs a third, and a casserole the fourth.

"Are they all for us?" Noelle asked. "I'm starving!"

"Mrs. Lloyd said she'd cook us *a* dinner—not four dinners," said Marie. "She has company coming tomorrow."

"So which is ours?" Noelle asked. "I know, the warm one. If she just cooked it, it'll still be warm."

"Smart thinking, Noelle!" Marie touched each dish. "Oh, they're all cold. Ethan? Ellen? Do you know what your mom wanted us to eat for dinner?"

"Maybe ice cream!" Ethan shouted.

"Cupcakes!" added Ellen.

"Could be, but I don't think so," said Noelle.

Marie thought back on her conversation with Mrs. Lloyd. Had she told Marie her dinner plans? Marie couldn't remember anything like that.

Suddenly, Marie knew how to figure out what Mrs. Lloyd cooked for dinner. And a bit later, she served a reheated home-cooked meal to her problem-solving assistants.

What's for Dinner?

How did Marie figure out what was for dinner?
Here's food for thought—the answer's on page 83.

A Yawn on the Lawn

Marie's friends catch her napping on the job. Will it cost Marie, or will her pals admit to joining her?

"I should've gone to bed earlier last night," Noelle said. "I can't keep my eyes open."

"Hey, you're the one who insisted we play best three out of five in that computer game," Marie said, stifling a yawn.

"Let's just ban computer games," Brooke said. "They're too addicting."

The girls leaned against the car windows as they rode to their Wednesday morning job. Mrs. Allen had loved the yard work they had done on their first job, so she'd hired them for the whole summer.

After they arrived at the house, the girls stumbled from the car, pulled out the hand tools, and mumbled "thanks" and "bye" to Mrs. Cantu.

"I'll mow in the back," Noelle said. "The noise will keep me awake." She walked into the garage to get the lawn mower.

"I'll grab Mrs. Allen's leaf blower and remove the bird-seed that falls onto her patio from the feeder," Brooke said. "That should keep everyone awake."

"And if you two plan to run those noisy machines in the back, I'll weed the front garden," Marie said. She hated loud noises—even from the other side of the house.

Marie slipped on her gardening gloves and knelt in the cool grass. She leaned into the garden and weeded, then yawned and weeded for about twenty minutes more. Finally, she removed her gloves and sat still for a moment, resting. She surveyed the yard, recalling all the hours they'd spent cleaning the yard the first week—it had needed much work after a long winter. But now the yard needed only minor upkeep: weeding, mowing, and patio cleaning.

Marie yawned again and thought, *Just for a minute.* She crawled under a tree and stared up at the deep blue sky through the branches. She soaked in the silence. The warmth. The gentle breeze. The blues. The greens. The peace.

And then, Marie was asleep.

"Sleeping Beauty! Oh, Sleeping Beauty! You won't find any princes around, so you need to wake up on your own." Marie felt someone nudge her side. She opened her eyes and saw Noelle and Brooke standing above her.

"Hey, Princess! Do you hear me? I've worked hard all morning and you've been napping!" Brooke said.

"Really!" added Noelle. "And I've pushed that mower nonstop. I begged for it to break down so that I could stop, but it kept rumbling on. And here you lay, asleep!"

"Let's dock her pay," Brooke joked to Noelle. "Does a quarter an hour sound perfectly fair to you?"

"Perfectly."

Marie sat up and yawned again. "Great nap. Worth every penny. But I won't be the only paying customer. I *know* you both didn't work the entire time."

A Yawn on the Lawn

How did Marie know that she wasn't the only one who had taken a break?

Don't get caught napping. The truth is on page 83.

A Lemonade Stand and a Business Plan

Marie's brother has high hopes for his lemonade stand. Will some older boys sour his business?

"That's delicious lemonade!" Marie said to her little brother, Chris. "You should make a lot of money."

"And when I do," said the boy from behind his stand, "I'll give you some money to buy me a present from Hawaii."

"Thanks, Chris," Marie said. She pulled a quarter from her pocket. "I'll be your first paying customer."

"I'll be your second," said Noelle. "I need a cold drink."

"So do I," said Matt. He and Russell and Nate walked up behind Noelle. The three boys went to school with her and Marie. "How much for a glass?"

"It costs $.25," said Chris.

"That's fair," Matt said. "You should make a little money. But how would you like to earn lots more money?"

"I want lots of money," said Chris.

"Of course you do," said Matt. "And I have a great plan. Now, listen. Who has more money? Little kids or big kids?"

"Big kids?" Chris asked.

"That's right," said Matt. "And the older the kid, the more money he has. But which kids are more careful with money? Little kids or big kids?"

"Big kids?" Chris suggested.

"Right again," said Matt. "And who can drink more?"

"Big kids?" Chris said again.

"Three for three!" said Matt. "Now, if I wanted a glass of lemonade, I'd think, *$.25 a glass? O.K.* I'll buy one glass, but only one because I'm careful with my money. But with a discount, I'd buy another one."

"A discount?" Chris asked.

"A cheaper price," Matt said. "Not for little kids—they drink only one glass anyway. But if I'm older, I might buy more."

"What's he talking about?" Noelle whispered to Marie.

"I don't know," Marie said. "But he's up to something."

"What's the right price?" Chris asked Matt.

"For every year old they are, offer that person a cent off the $.25 cost," said Matt. "I'm twelve. If you give me a penny off per year, I'd pay $.13. I'd think, *That's cheap!* And I'd buy lemonade for Nate and Russell, and another one for myself, then another two for Nate and Russell. Now, instead of making $.25 when you sell me one glass, you sell me six glasses and make $.78!"

"Wow! That's a lot of money!" said Chris.

"Soon the neighbors would buy it, and buses would stop, and sports teams would arrive, and you'd sell thousands of glasses! You'd be rich!" Matt shouted.

"Uh, Chris," Marie interrupted to save her little brother. "Is it fair to charge little kids more than big kids?"

"This isn't about 'fair,'" Matt said. "It's about business."

"Maybe it's about business," Marie said, "or maybe it's a plan to buy lemonade cheap. Either way, Chris won't make more money. In fact, with your plan, he'll lose money."

A Lemonade Stand and a Business Plan

What's the major problem with Matt's plan?
Turn to page 83 to cash in on the answer.

The Gentle Pony

Marie's friends convince her to ride a pony.
Will her puzzle skills land her in the safest saddle?

"You rode ponies?" Marie asked.
Mrs. Ferris had hired the girls to
help out at the Farmers' Market every
Saturday. But last weekend Marie had
caught a summer cold and had stayed home.

"We loved it!" Hope said. "You should see these
sweet animals, Marie. I wish my parents would buy me one."

"Where would you keep it?" Noelle asked. "The patio?"

"It's so sad you were sick," Hailey said to Marie loudly
enough for her mom to hear. "We need to take you riding."

"When things slow down," Mrs. Ferris said. "But let's
set up. I see customers arriving already."

"Yes, we're way too busy," Marie said quickly. She
organized the produce, moved over to work on the imported
odds and ends, and then jumped over to their homemade
crafts. "Don't just watch me. We have tons more to do!"

As the girls worked, the pony discussion continued.

"Ride a pony," Hope said to Marie. "You can choose
among four different ones, but ride mine. She's beautiful—
black and white. I love black-and-white horses. Both Polka
Man and Cookies and Cream are black and white."

"I'm not, uh, . . . *comfortable* with horses," Marie admitted.

"You're imagining large horses," said Noelle. "Ride a gentle pony and you'll be comfortable with it."

"I'll never be comfortable. Less than terrified, maybe."

"Oh, these ponies won't scare you," added Hope.

"No, thanks," said Marie.

"Face your fears," urged Noelle. "You tell us that."

"You won't leave me alone until I do," said Marie. She knew Noelle was right. "Which pony is the gentlest?"

"That would be the one that four-year-old rode," Noelle said. "She didn't want to ride, but the lady said it was a softy. I wouldn't ride that pony. It didn't *do* anything."

"That's the one I want to ride," Marie said. "The one that doesn't *do* anything. Which one was that?"

"Don't ride mine," Hailey said. "The one they call Gray Bones nearly bucked me off just because I scratched her behind her ears! I want to try Chocolate next."

"The brown one?" Hope asked.

"The brown one," Hailey answered.

"Which pony did the little girl ride?" Marie asked again.

"Just thinking about my pony's name makes me hungry," said Noelle.

"Excuse me," Marie said. "Which is the gentle pony?"

"Mine made me hungry, too," Hope said. "When does the snack bar open?"

"Never mind," Marie said to her friends. "I've figured out which one the girl rode, but thanks for your help."

The Gentle Pony

Which pony is the gentle pony? And how did Marie figure it out?

Trot to page 83 to find out.

Shake, Rattle, and Roll Over

Marie and Noelle love pet-sitting, until a stray shows up. Will the girls panic or put the dog in his place?

"Don't you love Ralphie?" Noelle asked. "He knows more tricks than we do!"

Mrs. Earl had hired Noelle and Marie to watch the Dalmatian while the Earls stayed at a lake cabin for the month. Every week Ralphie's trainer, Madeleine, stopped by to walk the dog to a nearby park for lessons. This week the girls tagged along.

Noelle and Marie watched as Madeleine ran Ralphie through his usual tricks: sit, stand, heel, shake, crawl, play dead, roll over, and speak.

"I have a new trick," said Madeleine. "Jump rope."

"Wow," Noelle whispered.

After Madeleine finished with the training, she invited Marie and Noelle to practice jumping with the dog. As the girls shouted out commands, an excited Ralphie showed his talents.

At the end of class, Madeleine hunched down next to Ralphie. She removed a blue metal charm from his collar and replaced it with a silver one. "You're moving up, Ralphie," she said, rubbing the dog's fur. "Before long, you'll wear gold!"

"Do you have a tight hold on his leash?" the trainer asked Marie.

"Sure," said Marie. "Why?"

Madeleine stood, smiled, and waved "good-bye" to Marie. Then, in a firm voice, she said, "Go home." Ralphie turned and raced toward his house, dragging a giggling Marie on the leash behind him.

Noelle dashed after them. "See you next week!"

Within minutes, the dog had slid onto the Earls' porch.

"Uh-oh, trouble," Noelle said, pointing to the garden.

A huge brown mutt sniffed and sifted through Mrs. Earl's tomato patch, ignoring the girls. "Think he'll fight with Ralphie?" asked Noelle.

"I doubt it," Marie said, "but we'd better be careful—"

Suddenly, before Marie could finish, Ralphie jerked the leash out of her hand and charged at the brown dog. The brown dog looked up, barked, and raced after Ralphie.

"Stop!" Marie shouted. "Ralphie, stop!"

But Ralphie didn't stop. He leaped at the other dog and put two front paws on the brown dog's side. Then the two dogs nipped at each other's necks. The dogs fell onto the lawn, wrestling and growling.

"Oh, no!" cried Noelle.

When the dogs heard Noelle, they stopped playing and turned to the girls, their tongues dangling in excitement.

"They're friends!" Noelle said.

"Who are you, big guy?" Marie asked.

"No name, but look!" Noelle pointed to a gold metal charm that dangled from the collar. "Madeleine's trained him."

"Hey, poochie. Where do you live?" Marie asked.

Ralphie jumped on top of the brown dog. After the girls laughed, he leaped on Noelle. "Down, Ralphie!" Noelle said. "Sit."

Ralphie sat. And so did the brown dog.

"See?" Noelle said. "Trained."

"Let me try something." Marie held out her hand to the brown dog and said firmly, "Shake."

The brown dog held out his paw. Ralphie held out his paw, too.

Marie stood up. "Roll over. Play dead. Speak." Both dogs obeyed each command.

"Madeleine *has* trained this dog," said Marie. "We could ask her where he lives, but we don't know where *she* lives."

"If Madeleine's trained him, then he knows her commands," said Noelle.

"And?"

"And he knows *all* of her commands," Noelle said.

"How does that help us?"

"You'll see," said Noelle.

Shake, Rattle, and Roll Over

How did Noelle find out where the brown dog lived?

Barking up the wrong tree? Turn to page 83.

Pisa and Sew Does

An elderly neighbor sends Marie a very odd message.
Is it an offer she can or can't refuse?

"We're halfway to Hawaii!" Marie announced. She'd added up the money they'd earned so far.

"Halfway to Hawaii is right in the middle of the Pacific Ocean," Noelle said. "How well can you swim?"

"Almost as well as I can earn money," Marie said.

"We can't count on digging up buried treasure every day," Noelle said. The girls had discovered Noelle's mom's stock certificates, just where Marie had said they would be. The stocks didn't make the girls rich, but their share did add a good chunk to their Hawaii fund.

"We have a month of summer left," Marie said. "And we'll figure out how to make money while we're in school this fall. By December, we'll be in Hawaii with lots of cash for souvenirs."

"Souvenirs! I'm bringing back pineapples," Noelle said. "I'm climbing the tree myself."

"Pineapples grow on plants, not trees," Marie said.

"Then I'll climb a banana tree and pick bananas."

"Bananas don't grow on trees, either—giant stalks."

"Doesn't anything in Hawaii grow on trees?"

"Coconuts," said Marie.

"Then I'll climb a coconut tree. I've always wanted to climb a tree in Hawaii."

"Since when?"

"Since just now."

"I'll climb something easier," said Marie, "like a mountain."

"Before you girls exhaust yourselves climbing," Marie's mother said behind them, "hike over to my computer. Mrs. Olson, from up the street, sent you an e-mail . . . I think."

"You think?" Marie asked.

"You have to see it," Mrs. Cantu said.

The girls followed Mrs. Cantu into her office. She showed them the e-mail, addressed to the girls:

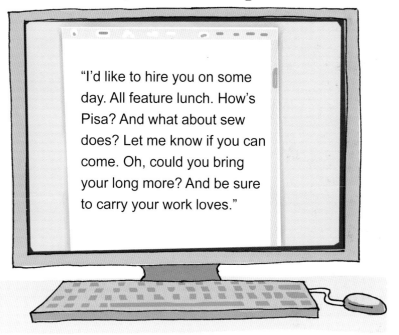

"I'd like to hire you on some day. All feature lunch. How's Pisa? And what about sew does? Let me know if you can come. Oh, could you bring your long more? And be sure to carry your work loves."

Marie and Noelle didn't speak. Then they said, "Huh?" in unison.

"How would we know if Pisa is O.K.?" asked Marie. "And I don't know anything about sew does."

"An all-feature lunch sounds good, but what's a long more?" Marie asked. "And what does she mean by 'carry work loves'? Does she want us to carry our work? She didn't even say what the work was or how much it would weigh."

"Are we sure it's from Mrs. Olson?" asked Noelle.

"Mrs. Olsen's arthritis is so bad, she can't type on a computer," said Marie.

"Just a minute," said Mrs. Cantu. "Mrs. Olson mentioned the other day that her son had a tool to help her use a computer. She speaks into the whatchamacallit, and it writes what she says or what it thinks she says."

"That's it!" Marie said. "Now it makes perfect sense!"

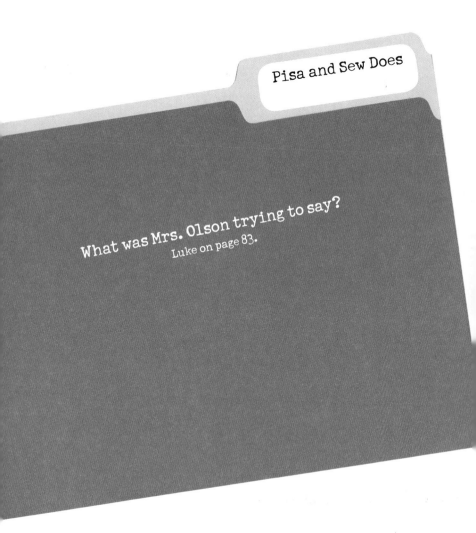

Pisa and Sew Does

What was Mrs. Olson trying to say?
Luke on page 83.

Luke on page 83.

Here's a Tip

Can money break up a long-lasting friendship?
Not if Marie has her way.

"Who would spend five dollars for one of these?" Noelle asked, placing a friendship bracelet on her knee. "Isn't that too expensive for a homemade bracelet sold at the Farmers' Market?"

"We have to pay for the beads and string," Brooke said, "so we're not asking as much as you think. And our time is worth something. Besides, people like to help out with a good cause. They won't mind paying."

"You're right," said Noelle. "But I don't know how many people would consider a Hawaiian trip a good cause."

Marie picked up another black bead from the pile in the middle of the kitchen table and slid it onto her string.

"You're taking all the oranges and blacks, Marie," Hailey said as Marie finished the string she was working on and tied the ends together.

"Halloween will be here in a few months," Marie said. "I figure someone might want to wear a cool bracelet then."

"I'm making a holiday bracelet, too," Brooke said. "I call it 'The Fourth of July.'"

"We celebrated that last month," Hailey said.

"But we Bostonians celebrate the spirit of the Fourth year-round," Brooke said. "Let me demonstrate." Brooke saluted and sang "Yankee Doodle" until the girls' groans and shoves stopped her tune.

"I'll tell you what kids like year-round," said Hailey. She held up her beaded string. "Lots of color. Some girl will see mine and beg her mother to buy it."

"Bet you can't guess what my color pattern stands for," said Sage, holding her string. Sage's beads repeated in a pattern of four different colors.

"The four seasons?" Noelle asked.

"I like that idea," Sage said, "but no."

"I like the idea, too," Noelle said. "Mind if I use it?"

"Go ahead," said Sage. "Give up?"

"We give up," the girls said.

"Each of these colors is the favorite color of a member of my family," said Sage. "Our family colors will hang on wrists everywhere."

"Won't it be exciting if these bracelets fly off the shelves tomorrow?" asked Noelle.

The next morning the girls set out the fruits and vegetables and spread out the exotic imported souvenirs. They placed their bracelets behind the fruits and vegetables, but Mrs. Ferris told the girls to move them to the front.

And people noticed.

Many shoppers who stopped bought bracelets, and even those who didn't buy any raved about the girls' creativity.

Eventually, a woman with a slight foreign accent stopped by. She had been eyeing the table for some time.

"How much for this?" she asked. She lifted a red, white, blue, and yellow bracelet into the sunlight.

"Five dollars," said Marie.

The woman inspected the bracelet. She smiled. "I'll take it. Did you girls make these?"

"Yes, ma'am," Marie said. "We all did."

"They're beautiful. Such nice friendships, no?"

"Yes," Marie replied.

"When I was ten, I had to leave my very best friend," said the woman as she reached into her purse. "She gave me a bracelet exactly like this and made me promise I'd never forget her. I haven't seen her since, but I've never forgotten our friendship."

The friends all looked at each other and smiled shyly.

"I want to give the girl who made this a tip." She pulled out an extra five-dollar bill.

"I made it!" Noelle and Brooke said in unison.

"I'm sure it was me," Noelle started, but Brooke cut in.

"No, I remember this one. It was mine."

"Mine!"

The woman stared at the girls. "I made a mistake," she said. "I didn't want to damage a friendship. Can you split the tip?"

"No need," Marie cut in. "I know who made this bracelet."

Here's a Tip

Who made the bracelet? And how did Marie figure it out?
Just "bead" it to page 85 to see.

Not Cool

It's a tie. Now Marie must choose between two plans.
Will her choice hurt three very close friends?

"We could hire skywriters," said Sage.

"If we were rich," said Rose. "But we can create a
mascot, Billy the Bully. The police could arrest him."

"How would we bring police to our school?" asked Hailey.

The girls sat on Noelle's back porch drinking lemonade
and brainstorming ideas for a citywide anti-bullying contest.
The winner would earn a $525 cash reward and a certificate.

"Why don't we just change our school's name to 'Friendly Elementary,'" added Hailey.

"Oh, much easier to do," said Rose sarcastically. "I hope Marie arrives soon. She has good ideas. Where is she?"

"She's entertaining visiting cousins," Noelle said. "But she'll be here. Besides, we can develop ideas, too."

"Let's ship all the bullies to Antarctica," Brooke suggested. "They'll be so cold that they'll promise to be good."

"O.K., so maybe we can't develop good ideas," said Noelle. The friends all laughed.

"Get serious," Noelle said. "We have a trip at stake."

"Maybe for you and Marie," said Hope. "But I plan to add to my savings for a new bike."

"School clothes for me," said Rose, raising her hand.

"A cute bedroom comforter," Sage chimed in. "Mine's still got ducks on it."

"I love ducks!" said Brooke. "In fact, I'm donating my cash to the animal shelter."

"I plan to surprise my mom with a special gift for her birthday," added Hailey. "It's coming up soon."

"We can't buy anything without a plan that will amaze the city," said Noelle.

"Let's do this!" urged Hailey.

The group agreed to focus on the contest instead of the reward. Brooke wrote every idea the team had into a notebook. After they had twenty ideas, Brooke read each one aloud. If the idea involved too much money or time, or too many people, the girls cut it. In the end, two ideas remained: a pencil promotion and a buddy plan. And then the team voted.

"Sorry I'm late," Marie said, bursting into the room. "My cousins just left. Any progress?"

"The good news," Noelle said. "We have two ideas."

"Awesome!" Marie cheered. "And the bad news?"

"Three voted for plan one. Three voted for plan two. That leaves you to break the tie."

"Bummer," said Marie. "Well, let's hear them."

"Plan one we call 'Buddies, not Bullies,'" Brooke said. "We team older kids with younger ones. Older kids read to younger ones, help with homework, and become their friends. Kids who have good friends don't usually bully others."

"Cool idea," said Marie. Noelle, Brooke, and Hope nodded enthusiastically. The three of them loved this idea.

"And the second?"

"We call plan two 'The Write Stuff,'" said Sage. She handed Marie a pencil.

Marie took the pencil and examined it. Sage had written from point to eraser:

TOO COOL TO BE MEAN

"The city prints a pencil for each student. The students see the slogan in class every day, and it begins to sink in," said Sage.

Hailey, Rose, and Sage felt strongly that this plan would fit the school's budget *and* be a big success with students.

Marie held up the pencil. She walked over to the sharpener on Noelle's desk, sharpened the point, and then said, "We should go with the buddy idea."

"We three like the pencil plan," Hailey said. "You're just siding with Noelle. Let's enter both ideas and see who wins."

"I like the idea, but it won't work," said Marie.

"It will," said Rose, "and we could use two chances."

"Yeah," said Sage. "If I have to stare at those ducks for much longer, I'll start quacking up."

The girls laughed at Sage.

"Just listen to me and then decide," said Marie. "I'm afraid the pencils will eventually send the wrong message."

Not Cool

What wrong message did Marie think the kids would get?

She proves her point on page 85.

Maze Craze

Marie and Noelle set the record for the corn maze. But will an ambitious group of kids steal their glory?

Yellow leaves, red apples, and orange pumpkins meant one thing to the kids in the town of Liberty: Mr. Clark's October Sky-High Corn Maze. And this year, Marie and Noelle landed much-desired positions at the farm—cornfield cadets.

"Left?" asked Noelle.

"No, I think right this time," Marie said.

Mr. Clark had heard about Noelle and Marie's Hawaiian trip and had asked the girls to help out during his farm's busiest hours. As part of their job, cadets had to study the maze until they knew it well enough to rescue a scared or lost customer.

The first few times Noelle and Marie entered the enormous maze, they wondered who would rescue them. But eventually, the girls memorized each turn, funny sign, and scarecrow. They knew when to turn right and when to veer left. They learned every cornstalk critter and every pumpkin-crafted animal in the maze: a rabbit, a camel, a reindeer, a giant frog, a turtle, and a rhinoceros.

After their fifth time through, Noelle said, "I think we could do this maze blindfolded."

"I think you're right," Marie replied. So the girls cut between the cornstalks and made a beeline for the entrance.

On opening day, the number of people who lined up to enter the maze surprised Marie. "Did you know the Sky-High Maze was this famous?" she asked Noelle on their first break. "I'm exhausted. How many kids have tried the maze so far?"

"I don't know. A gajillion?" Noelle said. "Heads up. Here comes another group. Back to work."

One at a time, the kids handed Marie their tickets. After a group gathered, she gave her usual speech: "Enjoy yourselves, scream if you get lost, and if you make it through in less than twenty minutes, you get a free pumpkin."

Then Marie marked the time on each ticket and passed it back.

"I'll win a pumpkin," said one boy, "to match my hat." He tugged an orange cap over his ears and ran to the maze.

Marie turned to Noelle. Her best friend's job was to mark exit times on the tickets. "What's been the fastest time yet?"

"Thirty-one minutes," Noelle said.

"It'll be tough to beat our record," Marie joked.

"Yeah," said Noelle. "But it took us five tries to get it down to eighteen minutes."

Marie turned and added entry times to more customers' tickets. During a lull, she asked Noelle, "Wanna try to beat our record over the next break?"

"Sure," Noelle said. "I'm tired, but not that tired!"

"Mark us!" shouted the boy with the orange hat. His group beamed at Marie and Noelle. "What's our time?"

Noelle checked their time. "Fifteen minutes. You beat our record. I didn't think anyone could do that!"

"Congratulations!" Marie said. "You're the new record holders. By the way, how did you like the cornstalk crocodile?"

"Way cool," said the boy in the orange hat.

"Scary!" said a girl with him.

"And didn't you love the pumpkin lion?" Marie asked.

"He nearly gave me a heart attack," said another boy.

"I liked the kangaroo best," Noelle said.

"It was O.K.," the orange-capped kid said. "But the lion was cooler. Now where are our pumpkins?"

"I'm afraid your team doesn't get a pumpkin," Marie said. "It's clear that you cut through the cornstalks."

"You're just jealous that we beat your time!" shouted one of the kids. "We want our pumpkin now."

"She's not jealous. She's right," said Noelle. "After two or three more tries, you might beat our record. But not this time."

Maze Craze

How did Marie and Noelle know that the kids hadn't beaten their time?

To find the answer, turn right, then left, then turn to page 85.

The Slogan Showdown

A slogan contest incites a battle of wills. Who will be a winner and who will be revealed?

"I don't know about you, but my brain's fried," Noelle said. She sat on a low branch of a willow tree in her backyard. Marie, Brooke, and Hailey lay on the lawn below.

"It's a $500 first prize!" Brooke said. "Think of something."

"We've thought of a hundred ideas," Hailey said. "None of them are any good."

After winning the school-district anti-bullying contest, the girls had entered every contest they could find. They hadn't won anything else, but they felt confident that eventually the perfect contest would turn up.

The perfect contest turned out to be one to create a new slogan for their town. Liberty hoped to attract new businesses and more tourists—and needed a good slogan.

"Let's take a break," Marie said. "Or at least find a change of location to inspire us."

"I know a great place!" Noelle jumped down out of the tree. "Our kitchen. Let's brainstorm and eat lunch."

The girls headed for Noelle's house. *SLAM!* went the back screen door as they entered the utility room that led to the kitchen.

"Sorry. Dad needs to fix that door spring," said Noelle. "Sandwiches?" she asked. Noelle pulled bread from a bread drawer and set it on the table. Then she leaned into the fridge and passed food to outstretched hands: roast beef, sliced turkey, mayonnaise, mustard, and peanut butter.

The girls created their sandwiches in silence.

Then Brooke offered, "How about, 'Give Me Liberty or Give Me Death!'"

"George Washington said that," said Nicholas, Noelle's brother, who entered the kitchen with his friend Colton.

"Actually, Patrick Henry said that," said Hailey. "It would make a gruesome slogan."

"Are you entering the slogan contest?" Nicholas asked. "We are, too! And as soon as we figure ours out, we're racing to the mayor's office and entering it. If two people come up with the same slogan, and it wins, the first one who entered it gets the prize."

"So, what's your slogan?" asked Nicholas.

"Like we'd tell you," said Noelle. "You'll race to the mayor's office and enter it as your own."

"We know when we're not wanted," said Nicholas. Come on, Colt." The two boys left through the utility room.

"Back to brainstorming," said Noelle. "We're close. I can feel it."

"Wait a minute," shouted Brooke. "I have an amazing idea! It's utterly perfect. How about—"

"How about we wait a second," Marie interrupted. She tiptoed to the utility-room door and yanked it open. Nicholas and Colton fell forward and crashed to the floor.

"Eavesdroppers," Hailey said.

"Nick!" Noelle shouted. "Out!"

"O.K., O.K.," said Nicholas. "We're leaving."

After the boys left, Hailey asked, "How did you know they had hung around, Marie?"

The Slogan
Showdown

How did Marie know?
If you're listening, the answer's on page 85.

What's at Steak?

A simple dinner out shows off Marie's problem-solving skills. Is she a cut above the rest?

Marie liked ridiculously salty steaks. She grabbed the saltshaker from the center of the table, sprinkled her steak generously, turned it over, salted the other side, and placed the shaker back.

"I can't believe you two leave tomorrow," Hope said. "You're so lucky!"

"A little luck, a great aunt," said Marie, smiling at her Aunt Kristine, "and a lot of hard work."

"And a prize-winning slogan that put you over the top," Brooke said. She'd been the one to think of their town's new slogan, "Come to Liberty, Where You're Free to Be Yourself!"

"And a prize-winning slogan!" Marie said to Brooke.

The girls had reached their goal. And as a going-away present, Marie's dad had invited the girls, their friends, and Aunt Kristine out to dinner.

"Take lots of pictures in Hawaii," Sage said.

"And remember everything," added Brooke. "I'll expect great stories and vivid details. I want to feel like I saw Hawaii."

"I wish you all could travel with us," said Noelle.

"Especially since your help made our trip possible," Marie said, slicing carefully into her steak. But after the first slice, she saw something she didn't like. "Darn!"

"No need to get upset," said Hailey. "We're happy you're going. Just send us a postcard."

"It's not that. It's—excuse me," Marie said to her passing waiter. "My steak is still pink."

"I'm sorry," said the waiter. "You asked for well-done." He picked up the plate. "I'll bring you a new steak right away."

Marie nibbled on bread.

"Are you touring all of the islands?" Hope asked.

"We'll probably spend all of our time on Oahu," Aunt Kristine said. "We'll find lots to do on that island."

"Have you visited Hawaii before?" Brooke asked.

"Aunt Kristine's traveled everywhere!" said Marie.

"Really?" said Hailey. "Where?"

Aunt Kristine started telling the girls about her travels just as the waiter set a steak in front of Marie.

"Your new steak," said the waiter. Marie cut off a small piece and put it into her mouth. "Perfect," she said.

After the waiter left, Noelle said to Marie, "That was nice of them to give you a new steak."

"Oh, it's not a new steak."

"How do you know that?" Noelle asked. "I don't see your cut."

"Oh, it'll be here somewhere," said Marie. She flipped over her steak. "See? Right here. Mmmm. Delicious!"

What's at Steak?

How did Marie know that this was her steak?
A really meaty answer is on page 85.

Sing Like a Bird

Marie and Noelle have helped lost kids, lost dogs, and lost causes. Now can they help a lost parrot?

"First stop, North Shore!" Aunt Kristine said to Marie and Noelle as the girls walked down the ramp at the airport.

Marie's chatty aunt had never stopped talking about the places she planned to take her niece and her niece's best friend. "So, are you ready for Hawaii?" she asked.

"Ready!" the two girls shouted as they pulled out their brand-new sunglasses.

"Off we go!" Aunt Kristine sang into the air as she pulled out onto the highway in her rented convertible.

Marie's aunt showed the girls her favorite sites, beaches, and stores. Everywhere they toured, the three visitors felt the spirit of Hawaii. They heard lots of *alohas* and *mahalos*. So far, a surf shop across from a school had turned out to be their favorite place. Brian, the young owner, shouted "Hang ten" to customers as he walked the girls through his shop, pointing out bodyboards, colorful T-shirts, waxes, and board leashes.

"I love your store," said Noelle. "May I take your picture?"

"It's cool. It's cool," Brian said. He posed next to a surfboard painted with a beach sunset.

"Could Aunt Kristine take a picture of Noelle and me on one of your surfboards?" Marie asked. She rushed to a demo stand.

"It's cool. It's cool." Brian left the girls to help a customer.

"I loved that store," Marie said, climbing into the car.

"We'll go back later," said Aunt Kristine. "We're eating lunch nearby. But first, I want to show you this fantastic art gallery. You girls will love it."

The gallery owner expressed that casual Hawaiian attitude. "Take your time. Life's too important to hurry," she said to the girls as they meandered among painted seas and carved dolphins.

"It must be relaxing to live here," Noelle said.

"I'd miss four seasons," Marie said, "especially the snow."

"They have snow in Hawaii," said Aunt Kristine. "On the mountaintops. You can even go skiing. Hawaii has lots to show you."

And show them it did. The sightseers hiked and explored. They shopped and browsed. And then they returned to Aunt Kristine's favorite café, which was packed with locals.

"That's how you know it's good," Aunt Kristine said.

After lunch, the trio strolled outside. "Look at that school," Noelle said, pointing to buildings across the street. "No halls! All the classrooms lead outside."

"The weather's nice enough that they don't need halls," Aunt Kristine said.

"Wonderful palm trees," Marie said. "And imagine seeing an ocean from your classroom. I'd stare out the window too often to ever finish studying," she added. "Look! The school even has its own parrot!" She pointed to the playground. Perched on the monkey bars sat a beautiful red-and-green bird.

"I must take a picture," Noelle said. She grabbed her camera and stepped closer to the bird. *Snap.* The bird didn't flinch. Noelle snapped another picture and inched even closer.

Marie and Aunt Kristine tiptoed up behind Noelle. The parrot jerked his head back and forth, watching the girls.

"I don't think this is a wild bird," Aunt Kristine said. "A wild bird would have flown away."

"Hey, bird," Noelle said. "What are you doing at this school?"

"It's school! It's school!" the parrot squawked.

"He talks!" Marie said.

"Now I really think he's lost," Aunt Kristine said. "He's probably flown away from his owner."

"It's school! It's school!" Now that the parrot was talking, he wouldn't stop.

"He's not lost," Noelle said. "He's telling us that he belongs here at the school."

"He's telling us where he belongs," Marie said. "But I don't think it's here at the school."

Sing Like a Bird

Where does the parrot belong?
Fly to page 85 to see the answer.

Treasure in a Bottle

Unsolved clues to a crime float into Marie and Noelle's hands. Can they solve their biggest mystery ever?

Marie and Noelle fell in love with Hawaii. They giggled as colorful fish rubbed against their legs in Hanauma Bay. They splashed in turquoise waters at Waikiki. And they tasted an amazing frozen pineapple drink at a pineapple plantation.

But after several days of being active tourists, they voted to do something different.

Nothing.

And the Dolphin Bay Resort—their hotel—was a fabulous place to do nothing.

As the three checked in, Marie said, "How can you afford this, Aunt Kristine? This is really fancy!"

"I know people," said Aunt Kristine.

"People like me?" a big man with a big smile asked. He walked up to Aunt Kristine and hugged her.

"Girls, meet my friend Joe Alisa," Aunt Kristine said. "He's made this hotel one of the best on the island."

"Oh," said Noelle. "You work here?"

Joe smiled. "But of course!"

"He owns the hotel," said Aunt Kristine. "We've been

friends since he was a surf shop clerk a million years ago."

"You worked your way up from clerk to hotel owner?" Marie said. "I'm impressed!"

"Yup," said Joe, laughing. "I own this hotel thanks to hard work—and my grandparents, who passed it down to me."

Joe insisted on escorting his three special guests on a tour of the resort. He showed them the pools, the enormous Kamehameha gym, the gift shop, the restaurant (where he treated them to lunch), the gardens that blocked the traffic noise of the Kamehameha Highway, and of course, the beach.

The only time during the tour that Joe didn't sport a big smile was for a brief moment when he led them through the hotel museum. He stopped at an empty display case.

"I wish I could get those back," he said. Joe told how just that morning, the staff had discovered the hotel's collection of antique shell jewelry to be missing.

"The pieces are rare and expensive," Joe sighed. "That's bad enough. But they've been in my family for 200 years."

Joe explained that he'd hired a young woman a week ago. "She said she was struggling to find work on the island. I felt sorry for her. Now the jewelry is missing and so is she."

When the tour ended, Joe smiled and told the girls to consider the hotel their home during their stay.

So on their day of doing nothing, they felt at home. The girls browsed through the hotel's gift shop and bought souvenirs for everyone—and two new swimsuits.

"Let's store our stuff in the gym lockers and try out our new suits in the pool," said Marie. "Pick a locker."

"Let's use 111. It's easy to remember," said Noelle. "And if we both memorize the lock combination, there's a chance one of us will remember it."

After their swim, the girls retrieved their locker contents and then strolled around the hotel in search of famous guests. "Is that Kate?" asked Noelle.

"No, but it could be Emma," said Marie.

Just when they thought they'd discovered all of Hollywood staying at their hotel, Aunt Kristine invited the girls to go beachcombing.

"I'd like to find a treasure map," Marie said. "Or a bottle with a message in it."

"You mean a bottle like that one?" Noelle asked, pointing to something bobbing in the surf.

"Why do people litter on such a pretty beach?" asked Marie. "There's a garbage can right there!"

"Yeah," said Noelle. "I bet it's not a bottle with a secret message or a pirate's map or anything."

The girls eyed each other, then sprinted into the water.

"Be careful, girls!" Aunt Kristine shouted after them.

Marie reached the bottle first. She held it up. "There *is* something inside!"

"No way!" shouted Noelle.

Marie carried the bottle back to shore and twisted off the cork.

The girls held their breath as Marie carefully pulled out a rolled-up piece of paper.

"What does it say?" Noelle said anxiously.

"Read it!" Aunt Kristine said. She was just as excited as the girls.

Marie unrolled the note and read it:

Shell jewelry.
212 Kamehameha.
Left 20, right 12, left 10.
Tell Joe at Dolphin Bay, HI.
I'm sorry.

"Is this what I think it is?" Noelle asked.

"Joe's stolen jewelry!" Marie said.

"Did the thief expect someone to find the bottle on this beach in front of the hotel?" asked Aunt Kristine. "Or did the culprit hope it would travel miles away?"

"Who knows how thieves think," said Marie. "But it'd be fun to find the jewelry for Joe."

Noelle and Aunt Kristine said that would be fun, indeed.

"Let's start at 212 Kamehameha Highway," Aunt Kristine suggested. The girls agreed, and they headed for the highway. They hiked along the road and discovered that 212 turned out to be a laundromat.

"Now," said Noelle, "do we go left for 20 paces or 20 feet?"

"And do we face the building or face away?" Aunt Kristine asked.

They tried every combination they could think of. Nothing made sense. They bumped into a building, a sign, the street. No place made a good hiding spot for stolen jewelry.

And then Marie stopped, smacked her head with her palm, and said, "We've been thinking about this all wrong. I know where the thief put the jewels."

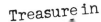
Treasure in

Pizza and Paradise

A table with jealous friends and a stolen slice—can
Marie solve both problems before the lunch hour ends?

Marie stared at the lunch choices—pizza with
applesauce and carrots *or* meat loaf with peas and a brownie.
The chocolate-frosted brownie looked delicious, but Marie
couldn't resist pizza. She headed for the pizza line.

After sniffing the fragrance of pizza all the way to her
table, Marie sat down with Hope, Sage, Faith, Hailey, Brooke,
and Rose.

Noelle trailed Marie and then sat next to her.

Before Marie could pick up her pizza, Hope said, "So,
tell us all about the trip. And be sure to include the shark that
chased you and your bad sunburn and how you couldn't enjoy
yourselves without us there."

It was the first day back at school since Christmas vacation and Marie and Noelle's trip to Hawaii. The girls couldn't wait to hear about their friends' trip, but the teacher had kept them busy. Now they finally had time to talk.

"It was paradise," said Noelle. "I'm so sorry!"

She and Marie told of their adventures, of the parrot, and of finding the stolen jewelry.

"In fact," Marie said as she picked up her pizza, inhaled the aroma, and prepared to finally bite into it, "our friend Joe was so grateful that he—"

"Uh, Marie," Noelle interrupted. She stood up at the table. "Can I talk to you in private?"

"Sure," said Marie. She held her pizza in the air a moment longer, about to take a bite.

"Marie!" urged Noelle.

"O.K." Marie put her pizza back on her plate, pushed away from the table, and walked into the hall with Noelle.

"What's up?" Marie asked.

"You're telling them about the Hawaiian trip Joe promised."

"And . . ."

"Our friends are so jealous, they're ready to switch tables. How will they feel when they find out Joe's invited us back?"

"When I'm done explaining, they'll be very happy. Now let's go eat."

Noelle paused for a moment. "What *could* you tell them? 'No need to help us earn money because this time it's free?'

Or, 'It's no big deal that we're going again—this time we'll bring back even better souvenirs?'"

"Good lines. Mind if I use them?"

"Marie!" Noelle shouted.

"Don't worry."

Marie rushed back to the table, a full two steps ahead of Noelle. She cleared her throat as she sat down. "As I said before, Joe promised us a . . . pizza?" She stared at her plate.

"Then he broke his promise," said Sage, who laughed along with the other girls.

"Yes, that's the trouble," said Marie. "Someone stole my pizza. My delicious pizza."

"Have some of my meat loaf," said Sage. "But don't touch my brownie."

"Or take a bite of my pizza," added Hope, holding out the slice on her plate. "But don't touch my brownie, either."

"Well, my pizza isn't big enough to share," said Brooke.

"Meat loaf?" offered Noelle meekly.

"In that case, I have two announcements," Marie said. "First, next Christmas, Noelle and I are going to Hawaii again. Joe gave us a free trip back for finding his antique jewelry."

The girls gasped.

"This time, I really *am* jealous!" said Hope.

"You don't need to be jealous," Marie said, "because I've talked to my parents and to Joe, and they said that all of you can come with us!"

After the screaming died down, Marie added, "You'll need to raise money for your airfare, but everything else will be covered. And Noelle and I can hook you up with some great jobs to cover your expenses."

The girls immediately began making plans.

Marie interrupted them, though, and continued. "I said I had two announcements. The second is" —Marie paused dramatically— "I know who took my pizza!"

The friends laughed as Marie picked up her slice and took a very big bite.

Pizza and Paradise

Who took Marie's pizza? And how did she know?
For a slice of the action, turn to page 87.